Angel

of the

Waters

Angel

of the

Waters

poems by

David Denny

SHANTI ARTS PUBLISHING
BRUNSWICK, MAINE

Angel of the Waters

Published by Shanti Arts Publishing

Designed by Shanti Arts Designs

Cover image: mrcmos / stock.adobe.com

Shanti Arts LLC
193 Hillside Road
Brunswick, Maine 04011
shantiarts.com

Printed in the United States of America

ISBN: 978-1-962082-09-9 (softcover)

Library of Congress Control Number: 2023948005

For Zach & Jesse . . .
my angels of mercy

CONTENTS

ONE

TWO

THREE

FOUR

FIVE

Am I a man who dreamed of being a butterfly,
or am I a butterfly dreaming myself to be a man?

—Soshi

I will complain, yet praise;
I will bewail, approve:
And all my sour-sweet days
I will lament, and love.

—George Herbert

ONE

AMONG WILDFLOWERS

A blanket of white English Daisies covers
the sprawling lawn at Three Oaks Park.

Ginny the Rescue Pup lowers her wet black
nose, bows to the daisies, snuffles, drops

into their scent, front paws first, then rear
haunches, laying her whole body elegantly

down like a coy courtier in the throne room
of a monarch, down she sinks into the grass

and the flowers. In her soft-as-rabbit ears
she hears Miss Emily Dickinson whisper,

The daisy follows soft the sun, a love poem
in which Dickinson likens herself to the smitten

flower, tracking her crush Samuel Bowles
across the morning sky. Ginny loves a good

tragic romance in which the beloved sails
westerly without pity or without recognition.

Although Bowles expressed polite admiration
for Dickinson's poetry, his eye was said to be

fixed upon her less literary, more attractive
and gregarious sister. Ginny of the long black

snout and the hairy moles and the bony deer legs
knows well how swiftly favor can shift from

the brilliant but homely rescue pup to
the expensive labradoodle with her pink bow

and the groomer's lavender scent upon her
fluffy tail. And so Ginny lay among *Bellis*

perennis, filling her nostrils and ruminating
upon the deep loneliness of her ilk, those

proletarian pups who can't resist the indelicate
sniff of fresh goose droppings. *Ah, love,*

Marvell cried, *let us be true to one another*
for the world, replete with grassy fields flush

with daisies that shimmer in the morning sun,
is also and nevertheless filled with clashing

ignorant armies and sun gods that warm
the morning fields without pity and without

recognition. In the distance, across the bejeweled
grass, gray squirrels flutter their tails, flaunt their

perky ears, and chip-chip with primal satisfaction.
No matter how fast Ginny the Rescue Pup flies

in their direction, they will in the final second
evade her passionate leap with a graceful curvet

up the bark of the big California Oak and
into the crux, where they taunt her with all

the bemused detachment of a lesser god,
dismissing her with a sly, smug twitch.

Botanical experts declare the English Daisy
a mere weed. Ginny knows well the old truism

that one person's weed is another's flower.
Having sampled the perfume of spring and

treed the upstart squirrels of Three Oaks Park,
Ginny the Rescue Pup proudly sidles up to

her human, his hand upon her shoulder a sign
that she blooms brightly in the field of his heart.

UPON THE MORNING

When Ginny the Rescue Pup awakens and
sniffs out a place in the grass to pee, when

she squats and looks to the orange tree,
watching the yellow jackets float from blossom

to blossom, when Ginny finishes her stream
and scratches the lawn with her back paws,

when Ginny puts her head down like a halfback
and bursts through the dog door, when Ginny

walks to her bowl and smells the morning meal,
when Ginny begins to tear and chew and chomp

and devour, then does Ginny begin to feel
the balance of her day unfold before her, and

as her belly receives nourishment, and as she
moves to the water bowl to lap and lap, and as

she bursts through the dog door again,
the plastic flapping in her wake, she stands

on the cool cement porch and lifts her head
and opens her nostrils and smiles her toothy grin

and welcomes the sky and follows the flight
of morning crows through camphor and sycamore

beyond her redwood fence, and as Ginny curls
into her spot in the shade and takes in a great

breath and blows it out like the blacksmith's
bellows, she knows with the certainty only

a dog can know, that whatever the day brings
is meant to be received with gratitude and grace,

with a wag and a lick, with a bark and a growl,
and when all three firetrucks roll from the corner

station at once, sirens calling to her, Ginny
the Rescue Pup stands at attention, lifts her chin,

once more draws in the sweet morning air, and
joins the neighborhood choir in its borning cry.

THE KIND ART OF DOMESTICATION

Above Three Oaks Park, a red-tailed hawk
circles. Ginny and her human lay in the cool

grass beneath a ring of crow-haunted sycamore.
She yawns, casually exposing her shark teeth,

unfurling skyward her long wet tongue, tasting
and approving the fine vintage of the wide world.

Her nostrils flare with 300 million receptors.
She snuffles and sneezes and insinuates her head

beneath her human's hand, craving stroke and
scratch and kiss, as the oxytocin spills into her

bloodstream, the result of generations of evolutionary
magic. Her strange cosmic love strangely includes

the clumsy bipedal oaf at her side, whose endocrine
glands respond in kind with a mildly euphoric buzz.

Although his hairy nostrils contain a mere 5 million
receptors, he nevertheless knows a good life when

he smells one, here beneath a ring of crow-haunted
sycamore and the beatific gaze of a red-tailed hawk.

AMONG GOPHERS

It's a nice day above ground but Ginny the
Rescue Pup keeps sticking her snout into

gopher holes at Three Oaks Park. She can smell
them down there in their moist, dark domain.

Ginny wants to meet the gopher queen.
She wishes to exchange the diplomatic nicety

of a good deep sniff and snort. The ancient
protocols never go out of style or lose their

cultural cachet. The gopher queen agrees;
she sends her emissary to escort Ginny through

the maze of tunnels to her throne room, where
she and her courtiers are eating popcorn and

turnips, which they freely share. The wormy,
loamy aroma goes to Ginny's head. She begins

to understand why the sun-shy feel so superior
to the clumsy bipedal oafs who tramp the grass

above. The treasure troves of the gopher
queen are filled with bulbs and tubers, roots

and daisies. Ginny blushes, realizing that she
has not brought a gift. All she has is her red

collar with her metal name tag. As she bows
to kiss the monarch's razor claws, she offers

the shiny tag. Your Highness, she humbly
intones. The queen holds the tag close to her

dark eyes. On one side Ginny's name appears
in letters longer than a gopher's tooth.

On the other side is her address. You may
visit any time, she tells the queen. We have

a luscious backyard with tasty flowers all
around its perimeter, not to mention a young

pear tree with long fresh roots. Tell me what
you know, the queen inquires, of the giant

creatures above with ugly feet and hairless bodies
that emit strange yeasty odors. They are most

odoriferous, Ginny admits, and they treat their
own kind with the same artless violence that

they approach all creatures. But I have known
a few who have tenderly stroked my ears

and belly, all the while cooing my name
and praising my beauty. Such beings must

be viewed with pity and approached, if
approach you must, with tiny timorous steps.

Squinting as she emerges, Ginny pauses
to consider the elegance and the opulence

of the Gopher realm. There are those above
ground who see them as a nuisance, setting

vicious metal traps that skewer or strangle.
But Ginny the Rescue Pup dreams of a day

when the traps are melted into name tags for all,
and the bounty of the world's gardens are shared

equally with all creatures, insects, birds, even
clumsy bipedal oafs who reek of meat and bread.

OF THE SPHERES

As Ginny the Rescue Pup pauses to smell
the purple spears sprouting from the butterfly

bush, she sneezes, and then apologizes to
the bees, who scatter now in the midday calm,

reconvene, and resume their cosmic chore.
The work of pollination is the work of angels,

after all, in whose quivering wings we find
all we need to know of the world's quantum

machinery. Ginny passes in turn to the jasmine,
the lavender, and the rosemary, her black wet

nostrils flaring from bush to bush. A few blocks
away fire trucks roll from the station: one-two-three,

engines belching from gear to gear; their
sirens leap into the air, calling to Ginny

who opens her throat, extends her jaw, and finds
their key: one-two-three-four. The air fills with

the harmony of this quartet, and the chord they
forge brings momentary peace upon all beings.

As the sirens fade into the afternoon, Ginny
lowers her head in gratitude. The sweet scent

of utter silence fills the air as Ginny the Rescue Pup
inhales, filling her lungs with all our troubles,

then slowly exhales, releasing them, relieving all our
burdensome woe, all our bedeviled and misguided noise.

NEWS OF THE FLAGGING WORLD

Each day now spring brings something new
to the pond. Lately the lilies have opened wide,

and the painted ladies have begun their
brief reign. Ginny strolls down the sidewalk

to the cool rhythm of Miles Davis at Newport—
young Miles with his bell right on the microphone

and the audience enthralled. Her sleek nails
click time on the concrete. She stops to sink

her nose into a tall clump of lush grass. There
she reads the daily news in the fragrant urine

of the goldie down the street or the Maltese
from two blocks over. She squats and adds

her own liquid paragraph. Then she scratches
her byline with all four paws, lifts her head,

and prances on—now rolling to the rhythm
of Stevie Wonder, hips in sway, snout held high,

her glistening nostrils flaring with morning ardor.
Not all the news is good, but it's not all bad either.

Today she knows how many fuzzy goslings
she will find among the Canada Geese when

she arrives at the pond. She tunes her pipes
to the key of life with a sharp bark in the general

direction of two crows clicking and cawing
her name from the sagging telephone wire.

AMONG SWALLOWS

On Ginny the Rescue Pup's grassy field, barn
swallows swoop and glide three feet off the

ground. Unable to restrain herself, Ginny
gives chase. Her fine thin muscled legs gallop

like a racehorse; her tongue joyfully lolls
as the wind blows back her floppy ears.

"Ground effect" is the aerodynamic advantage
to flying low, something the swallows know

and relish. Ginny keeps pace, as the swallows
lead her just beyond reach. O, Ginny, you

happy-go-lucky poocheroo, skimming across
the green green grass! Squirrels and crows

watch with awe and envy from the nearby stand
of Monterey Pine. Watch that Ginny-girl go!

At the end of the field the swallows angle,
divide, and turn; Ginny isolates one bird, barks,

and reverses course in tandem; both bird and
dog resume chase speed until the swallow lifts

and banks and finally leaves the field for
the pond. Ginny watches the swallows go.

Like a prize filly turning back to the stable,
she trots to her human, laps water from her jug,

and crunches up a biscuit treat. The joy in her
visage shines through the rest of the day.

Back home, she lounges upon her couch like
Cleopatra upon her barge. Sailing upriver,

a Judean girl paints her nails. Queen she is
of the Nile, a goddess upon her throne,

napping while mortals on the shore pick her
fruit and hunt her meat and bake her midday meal.

The Mycenaean servants sprinkle pink petals
upon her tawny fur. Palm fronds in the canopy

are proud to shelter her from the sun's peasant
rays. Beneath her barge's wake, fish contend

to bite her royal fisherman's bait. Ginny the
Rescue Pup reigns with graceful munificence.

ON THE POND

From the relative safety of tall sycamores,
a pair of crows hector Ginny the Rescue Pup.

She gazes up at them; they rattle and caw
their objections to her presence. She answers

with a single bark before she strolls around
the corner and over to her pond, where bright

orange dragonflies and green hummingbirds
dance over the surface of the water, arousing the

interest but not the ire of mother and father Mallard
with their seven ducklings in tow. It is another

marvelous morning at the pond as Ginny sits
in the shade, ruminating, as she often does,

upon the simple joys of earth and sky, air
and water. A pair of barn swallows swoop in

and glide in precise formation over the surface
of the pond. Ginny feels her predatory impulse

arise along with the fur on her back. She breathes
deeply, filling her lungs slowly from bottom to top.

She lay between boulders, crossing her paws.
Let the swallows be swallows, she thinks,

and let the ducks be ducks, and the trees
be trees, and the sky be merely sky. She feels

the wind in her ears; jasmine fills her nostrils.
Somewhere in the distance geese can be heard

honking directions home. Ginny the Rescue Pup
closes her eyes and attends to their doleful song.

TREASURE ON THE FIELD AT DUSK

Ginny sidles up to a pile of still-warm deer scat,
like a miniature stack of fragrant cannonballs—

misshapen cannonballs, knocked-aside and rejected
cannonballs, of-no-use cannonballs. She lifts her head

to see where the deer have gone. She would like
to run with them. They have left behind only

their musky scent, and this loose stack of rich scat,
dropped with a casual twitch of the white tail.

Ginny lowers herself to the grass, rubs her muzzle
and neck in the scat, rolls in it, marking herself,

should they return, as one of their kind, a sister
of their imperious, lanky, and long-legged herd.

AMONG PHILOSOPHERS

Ginny the Rescue Pup has read her Schopenhauer
and believes him, in part, when he writes that

the Intellect is a lame man who rides upon
the shoulder of the blind giant Will. Ginny is

usually dubious of binary suppositions,
favoring paradox and mystery over reductionist

certainty. (She is Belgian Shepherd, after all,
not German—Underground Resistance Fighter,

not Nazi Storm Trooper.) But indeed there are days
when, in the spirit of Schopenhauer, she snarls

and growls at the world, which seems ever worthy
of contempt, though it merely wants to pat her head

and kiss her long black snout. Surely there is
more to mammals than Intellect and Will. What,

for example, about this strange little mongrel
the Heart, softened by beauty and by love?

Surely even Herr Schopenhauer felt stirrings
that challenged the limits of his rational vocabulary.

On certain summer mornings, when a breeze
flows in from the bay, whisking the redwood needles

high in the sunlit crowns above her pond, Ginny's
blind giant settles in the shade beside the water,

while her lame one props against a boulder and
contemplates the orange dragonflies flitting to

and fro over the surface, the Mallard couples
sliding down over the small waterfalls, mayflies

swirling on columns of warm air, bright green
hummingbirds feeding greedily on lupines.

On such summer mornings her giant, whose
nerves are usually abuzz with anxiety, seems to

surrender his urgency. He shrugs and releases
the muscles of his neck and shoulders, inflamed

by the burden of the malformed one who must
ride in order to see. And her lame one describes

for her giant the tranquil flow of water from
the two upper ponds, which empty into the

expansive central pond, which empties into the
lower pond that sprouts with two musical fountains.

On a boulder at the edge of the lower pond sits
a child's firetruck, cast aside one winter's day,

left to rust in the spray of the fountains, an image,
Herr Schopenhauer might say, of alienation.

Just so, here we sit upon our little blue planet
twirling under the spell of the sun in a vast

and otherwise dark cosmos, abandoned, heartbroken—
yet we bear witness to irreducible Mystery,

to a scene we can only describe as beautiful
and only feel as, well, love. In such musings

Ginny the Rescue Pup hopes to overcome
the binary supposition that divides rescuee

from rescuer, to resolve, or at least transcend,
the flagging world's troubled and divided spirit.

WITH THE BEATLES

Ginny the Rescue Pup grows impatient with
John's wobbly politics. She indulges Ringo's

rhythmical hijinks. Fond of a good melody,
she can bring herself to hum in the key of Paul.

But it is George—soulful George, furry George,
hippy George—that she loves. She is a joyful

pooch and likes a good romp as much as any;
however, life, for her, is serious business,

fraught with danger and deceit, and over much
too quickly. Like George, she thinks there is

something to this Unity of All Creatures that
underscores our doggy lives, great and small,

ugly and cute, something vast and mysterious,
cyclical and cosmic that her canine spirit laps up

like the choicest broth-soaked kibble with carrots
and peas on top. On her annual pilgrimage to

Friar Park, Ginny loves to pee at the feet of George's
gnomes, and wander his estate, and bark at the

statue of George's dog, and offer her ears to
George's widow, and breathe the air that George

once breathed. In the shade of George's gazebo,
Ginny the Rescue Pup naps, then drinks from

his spring. On the gentle breeze her beloved's
guitar still and always weeps and weeps and weeps.

AVOIDING THE FATE OF OLD TIRESIAS

When the wild turkeys come gobbling through
Ginny's neighborhood, she feels compelled

to round them up, make them her flock by
herding them to a corner of the grassy field

that offers no escape. Why do they resist her
kind tutelage? All she wants is to school them

in the art of the gangly strut and the harmonic
cluck. But her bark is misinterpreted. Good for Ginny

that they scatter and flap for the rooftops and tree
branches; turkeys have been known to pluck the eyes

of those that threaten their young. Waiting for them
to come down from their roost, she soon grows bored

and thirsty. And so she meanders home, in her own
sweet way, to her napping spot in the shade,

where the green hummers descend to suck nectar
from the pale pink hollyhocks, and where her human,

that gentle oaf, refills her water bowl and tosses
turkey-flavored treats into her waiting jaws.

AMONG IMPRESSIONISTS

Ginny the Rescue Pup breaks through the edge
of a lavender field and crosses a dirt road.

She ventures up a hillside and into cypress trees
where she finds Paul Cezanne at his easel.

Yet again his gaze is fixed on Mont Sainte-
Victoire in the hazy blue distance. She likes

the mountain too. Ginny lays down in the grass
and takes up Cezanne's view. She watches him

work some cobalt into his sky. He takes a step
back and swears a streak of words she has not

heard since her time in the Montmartre whorehouse.
He throws his brush into a patch of geraniums

some twenty feet away. He holds up his hands
before his face as if they are foreign objects.

How and when had these clumsy useless things
attached themselves to his wrists? He wipes them

on his trousers, already splotched with terra verte,
and shakes them, hard, as if trying to detach

ligament from bone, then smacks his palms
together until they turn red. Finally, Cezanne

sinks into his chair, pulls his tobacco pouch
from his pocket, and stuffs his pipe. He smokes

until the scowl on his forehead unfolds itself.
He gazes at the mountain until he is able to see it

clearly once again. You can look at a thing
all your life, thinking you know it, and then

the light changes, the wind shifts, your eyes
find a new focal point, and suddenly it appears

whole for the first time. Ginny rests her chin
upon her crossed paws. So much psychic energy

is wasted by humans in their tantrums. Artists
and monks are especially prone to self-abasement.

If only they could howl. In such a way, divine
grace fills the air and settles the blood. Cezanne

disappears into the corner of his house. He emerges
a moment later with a plate of food scraps—

chicken and turnips. He sets the plate in the grass
in front of Ginny. He strokes her head and

scratches her ears. She opens her nostrils so as
to share his tobacco smoke. One must love a human,

even a sour-tempered human, who smells of tobacco
and knows how and where to scratch. There you are,

pretty girl, Cezanne coos. You must be hungry
tramping around Provence in this heat. There is

fresh flowing water in the creek there just
beyond the trees. Take some water, love, and

rest here long as you like. You have brought me
luck, sweet pup, and rescued my morning.

He takes up a fresh brush, dabs and draws it
through the oils on his palette. Ginny eats

the master's food and dozes in his grass. When
she awakens, Cezanne's painting is almost finished.

Ginny the Rescue Pup ambles to his side, opens
her throat, and releases a celebratory howl.

Cezanne sets his pipe aside, tilts his head
back, opens his throat, and matches pitch.

IN HER DREAMS

When Ginny the Rescue Pup sleeps she whimpers;
her paws twitch; her eyeballs switch back and forth

beneath her eyelids. In her dream she is barking
and chasing a flock of swallows who skim

the surface of a grassy elysium field just ahead
of her flaring nostrils and lolling tongue. O,

she is wild to catch them, though some part
of her knows she never will, for Ginny

is all about the chase. At the edge of the field,
the swallows, like fighter jets, slow and bank

and turn, heading back full steam across
the open field. Ginny pivots and turns, gallops

after them on her skinny racehorse legs,
the ultimate canine machine, tuned and oiled,

her straight body in perfect line behind her
sensational snout. The field is her runway.

When she takes flight and joins the swallows
in the air, it seems a natural progression.

Together they fly to Ginny's pond and skim
the surface together. Ginny lifts on her

new wings and soars above her flock.
She circles the pond and returns to the field,

which has now become her landing strip.
When Ginny the Rescue Pup touches down

she pants and smiles and drinks and takes a
luxurious roll in a fragrant pile of goose poop.

THE UNKIND CRAFT OF DOMESTICATION

When she spots the white-tailed bunnies munching
grass in front of the hydrangeas, Ginny lifts her

front paw, stiffens her body; she is cocked and
pointed, like an arrow stretched in a taut bow.

One quiet and careful step at a time, she stalks
her prey. The clumsy bipedal oaf who holds her

leash locks it with his thumb so she cannot
charge and jerk his spine all out of whack.

Hearing the click, she sinks to the grass, heaving
a pent-up sigh. Saliva drips from the edges

of her mouth. Her shark teeth ache with yearning
for all the forbidden things beyond the leash's length.

AMONG THE HEAVENS

Ginny the Rescue Pup first fell in love with
the moon when she lay in a cardboard box

in a Fresno orchard with her four abandoned
siblings. As the others slept, she saw through

the trees the glowing orb up there just beyond
the leaves. It shone down upon her, soothing her,

taking the place of mother, as it slowly moved
across the night sky. On many a night since,

she has lain in the moist grass of her backyard
and watched the clouds play peek-a-boo with her

sky mama, obscuring and revealing like a cosmic
magic trick. Now she sees her, now she doesn't.

A big dog now, she knows that it is merely
a big gray rock, orbiting her home planet,

reflecting back the light of the sun. Yet in its
cosmic silence it calls to her. One night Ginny

dream-books a flight on a SpaceX rocket.
For a price, the capitalist astronauts buckle her

into a pod and send her for a sleep-over on the
dusty/rocky surface of the moon. There she romps

in her baby blue spacesuit, pees on the stars and
stripes, chews on a golf ball, curls up for a nap on

Neil Armstrong's space boots. She is surrounded
by space junk, some cool stuff—camera lenses,

moon buggy tires, bags and bags of human poo.
Kinda nice to nuzzle with sky mama at last.

Kinda lonely though. Kinda cold. Kinda sad
if you really wanna know. In the morning her

bright blue planet bursts upon the horizon
just as the SpaceX capsule returns for her.

On the long ride home, Ginny gets a window seat
and a bowl of her favorite freeze-dried kibble.

She sucks Gatorade through a long straw, snoozes
off and on, dreams of chew-bones and grassy fields,

squirrels and sparrows. Through her porthole
there is plenty to see—blinking satellites and star

trails, slow asteroids and fast comets. But she finds
it hard to take her eyes off the looming blue globe.

Each time she awakens, the earth takes up more
and more space in her window. How lovely

my home, she thinks, with its orange dragonflies
and green hummingbirds, its humans who share

their tobacco smoke and praise even her simplest
tricks, its dance movies and bebop jazz, its

honking geese and howling sirens. Ginny
the Rescue Pup can hardly wait for the fiery

reentry, the thundering boost-back burn
landing, the cheers of the welcoming crowd.

AT THE BROWN DERBY

Ginny the Rescue Pup strolls into the famous
restaurant on the arm of Fred Astaire. Although

he is now in his 70's, the elegant hoofer still
carries himself with dignity and grace. And

of course he's dressed to the nines. All eyes
are drawn to him as the hostess guides Ginny

and Fred to his regular booth. The bartender
appears with Fred's standing order of a Martini

with three olives. Ginny orders a Shirley Temple.
When the waiter appears, Fred orders them each

a Cobb Salad and Crepes Suzettes. William
Holden and Cary Grant stop to visit for a moment

on their way out. One of MGM's old stage crew
knocks hello on the table as he passes. Fred

explains how the gentleman had been of service
back in the days when Fred danced up walls

and across ceilings. He was the man who brought
buckets of ice water just off camera for Fred

to soak his feet. Outside, in the glaring Southern
California sunshine, Ginny knows exactly

how many rats nest up in the crossed palm trees
that arch over the entranceway. Of the cars

passing on Hollywood Boulevard, she knows
Rolls from Ford, Porsche from Datsun. After

Fred leans down and kisses her snout, he climbs
into his Jaguar. Ginny the Rescue Pup strolls around

the corner to order two hot dogs from the street
vendor. Extra mustard. Slab of sauerkraut.

SAINT JULIAN AND THE RESCUE PUP

Ginny harkens to the nightly horn of the freight train
as it rumbles past, alerting all beings within

earshot that it's eight o'clock and all's not exactly
well. Darkness has fallen; the streetlamp's glow

alights the row of filthy silver cars such that
Ginny pauses her constitutional to consider

the graffiti and muse upon how much and how
little the world has changed since Whitman's

locomotive "launch'd o'er the prairies wide."
This one scuttles through suburban backyards,

interrupting children's bedtime rituals with
the low keen of doomed empire. Echo it will,

this lonesome lament, unbidden, all through their
adult lives, even as they pledge their allegiance

to our shabby anthem of never-ending commerce.
Soon the train passes. Ginny raises her head

to the silent stars as they wink their death throes,
invoking the chirr of the first summer cricket.

And then another. And yet another. Until the insect
choir billows the dark with joy recovered: all is

well, all will be well, indeed all manner of things
in heaven and earth will be unequivocally well.

TWO

SUBURBAN HOURS

Sunrise

Just before dawn a family of raccoons
crosses the street in front of me and
disappears down the drain beneath the curb—
a mother and two youngsters. Their descent
into the fecund underworld becomes
the focus of my morning meditation.
I imagine their journey to the bay
illumined by streaks of daylight from above.

Suddenly, loping down the middle of the road,
comes a coyote with a rabbit in his jaws.
This bold one steals my thoughts from me.
Morning clouds appear with a reddish glow.
Over the frosted rooftops comes the sun!
How can we judge the living and the dead,
we who stroll among the cul-de-sacs of
imagination in search of morning blessing?

Early Morning

The warm summer sun has already begun
to steal the dew from the front lawn.
I surprise a red-tailed hawk stripping
a large pigeon of its feathers, the gray

and white puffs blowing like a tide around
the cement driveway, clinging to oleander.
The hawk grabs the corpse in its beak and
attempts to fly. The pigeon is too heavy.

He drops it and retreats to the neighbor's
rooftop, then again retreats to his perch
in the tall pines. I beg his pardon and
leave the broken-necked pigeon where it lay.

An hour later I return. Only the feathery
wisps remain, and those, even those, will be
collected by the squirrels to pad their nest
high in the heart of the holly oak.

Mid-morning

On my way into church, the deep summer
smell of jasmine stops me. But it's the delicate
green hummingbird that holds me in place
as it works the star-shaped blossoms
one by one. Deep inside the bush, bees
too, are working to the steady buzz of their
tiny motors. My senses fill to the brim,
then overflow. Lord, don't they overflow!

In the text for today, a raven revives the spirit
of the prophet Elijah. I am no prophet,
but I've got this darting hummer here, whose
clarion wings swing low like a heaven-sent
chariot, calling me to worship, and I've got
this sweet scent of arousal and awakening
that sends a shudder through my rigid soul.
Lord have mercy, don't it shake me though!

Noon

I park my car at the curb and sit alone
beneath the holly oak where yesterday
a squirrel launched from this curb too soon,
got caught beneath the tire of a neighbor
dropping off his child at the middle school.
Watching from the wires, the crows waited
until the morning traffic cleared then
descended to take their slow samples.

Beyond the shadow of this oak, the remains
cling to the asphalt, stuck in tar and blood.
Today acorns drop on my windshield.
Another squirrel is at work in the tree.
By eternity's reckoning, one day is very like
another: the leaves turn and tumble,
the acorns fall where and when they will.
I close my eyes and listen to their rhythm.

Afternoon

The knotted trunk of the big holly oak
in my front yard reaches straight up for ten feet
before it splits into five stalwart branches,
five elegant fingers pointed skyward.

Varied and constant is the birdsong.
The squirrels nest high enough to sway
in summer breezes that sweep up from the bay.
Grubs and insects, yes, by the zillions.

Acorns thump my car like a jazz drummer
who can't decide between brushes or sticks.
Nature's city in the sky—this marvel,
this descendant of the Tree of Life.

Come, sit with me on my front porch.
From the green bench beneath the eaves,
watch with me all the comings and goings,
listen to the chatter and the twitter,

the creak and groan of the great branches,
this universe that spans the yard,
guarding our little house from sun and rain.
When the crows begin to caw and rattle

and the squirrels chip-chip their way
on branches too slim it seems to hold them,
we will cross our legs, you and I, meekly
sip our tea, and gaze up in wonder.

Sunset

A red fox makes her way across my fence line,
then drops down into the neighbor's yard,
down the slope of their rotted plum tree.
Her fidgety kits follow, curious but obedient.
Snipping at each other's heels, they follow.
The mother settles them into their den—
one first, in her gentle jaws, then the other.
And me, I settle myself into a lawn chair,
watch the clouds redden with sunset;
the deep blue sky yields to zillions of stars.

Earlier in the week, I discovered a blood
puddle at the foot of my driveway; wisps
of stuck fur waved in the morning breeze;
bright spots trailed along the suburban street.
Two houses down, the blood veered from
asphalt to sidewalk to grass—there,
a flesh-stripped corpse on the neighbor's lawn,
head and spine and tail intact. Fixed eyes
stared out, torso eaten clean. Not my cat.
First thought: coyote or mountain lion.

This evening's second thought: red fox?
Inside, my cat pleads, her dish empty.
Behind the safety of glass and screen,
her stomach cry, a call to her primate kin.
The slider squeals open like worn car brakes.
Twining around my ankles, the cat cuffs them
with her claws, exposes her soft underbelly.

I slide closed the door to our den, lock us in—
the darkness outside a staging ground
for bloodshed; the light inside, our only solace.

Midnight

When I turn my car onto the dark street,
a great horned owl swoops across my windshield.
Her gray-white wingspan glows in the headlights.

In my mind, she excises the spirit from my body,
and in her talons I soar through the night sky,
over rooftops and into the tall Monterey Pine.

Friend, what predatory magic would
you teach me? I whose scavenger heart
seeks only easy prey, and from whose throat

come only caws and clicks and rattles—
domestic noises uttered in broad daylight
in the shade of a homely curbside oak.

What new liturgy might we recite to
the moon, that heavenly aspergillum,
sprinkling its light among the branches?

WILDING

We had a cat and called her Molly.
She tangled our feet for nineteen years.
Queen of the backyards and the front,
she brought us rats and jays and wrens.
One day she carried a squirrel indoors.
Furious with us when we shooed it out,
she punished us with glare and yowl.
Once she stood on hind legs to tear
at tufts of a dog's fur with front claws.
She climbed and leapt and roamed and howled.
Reach to pet her and she'd wrangle your hand,
take it in her jaws, and threaten muscle
from bone. She'd purr and slide her downy
length along our jeans until we pet her from
nose right down her spine to tail tip.
Queen of the backyards and the front,
we had a cat and Molly was her name.

GAGGLING

Four geese come honking
low over my house,

as they descend toward
the middle school soccer field.

Were I ancient Roman,
they would be an omen.

But I am modern American,
and they are only geese

negotiating a place to land.
Yet I might say this much:

the children's cleats churn
goose poop into the soil,

creating a pungent green
runway to the future,

about which their parents
honk a chorus of regrets,

as they watch their young
stretch their necks and flap

their untested wings into
the dappled and unruly sky.

OPEN LETTER TO THE WATCHERS

The bulbous spider in the corner of the window
waits out the sun, grows fat on shadows.

Scattered about her web, detritus neatly wrapped—
bits of moth, fly, gnat, ant, silverfish.

A plump rat on his back in the side yard—
did he fall from the roof or did he eat our poison?

I am glad to seal him in a baggie either way
and drop him in the garbage at the curb.

I have learned to count the bare branches
that criss-cross in front of the winter moon.

And when in spring the pink blossoms burst
along their length, I hope to observe the squirrels

who devour them whole, one by one. Where
you live, how do your lonesome days pass?

ALL AND NOTHING

The lean spider whose web stretches across
the corner of my bathroom window has poisoned
and wrapped a plump June bug for later consumption.

Because she tucks herself into the shaded
window frame, I rarely see her in daylight.
By night I often see her silhouetted in moonlight
as she repairs the daily damage to her web
and nibbles at her leisure on her prey.

Morning sunlight illuminates water droplets
on the windowpane, turning them into mini
spotlights that throw rainbow colors onto the tile.

Some days I am the spider. Others, I am the June bug.
Some strange mornings I am indeed the web.
There have been rare times when I am
the sunlight refracting the droplets. And even
rarer times when I am the moon's glow.

Someday soon I will be all of them at once, and more—
also I will be nothing at all, not even the breeze
that shimmies the tattered threads of the spider's web.

PASSING PARADE

When my wife dies, she wants to be cremated,
but not before donating any and all useful organs.
She wants her body to do some good when
she has no more use for it, and then she wants it
to take up as little space as possible with her
modest cremains. She doesn't understand
my desire to be buried when I die. I suppose
it is selfish of me to prefer the tradition of my
ancestors, leaving the body, such as it will be,
intact, undonated, and lain in a pine box,
a waste of space and a waste of perfectly good wood.
I've always preferred soil to flame. A backyard
gardener and longtime lover of grassy fields
and flowers, trees and birds, butterflies and creeks,
I want to contribute to the soil with the help
of time and worms, insects and other critters
involved in nature's great recycling project.
I'd like to be buried in such a setting, with
a stone marker that bears my name and dates.

My wife, when she dies, wants a choir of children
to sing happy songs at her memorial service.
I've told her that, if I have the bad fortune to
be present, I will share her favorite joke. I think,
for myself, I prefer a brief funeral rite, with words
of hope and grace spoken by a pastor, and maybe
a hymn or two about the beauty of the earth and
her way of yielding, nurturing, and embracing us.

Let my family and friends, if any yet remain,
tell stories and read poems over drinks in the corner
of a friendly local pub where people regularly gather
to share the warmth of their kind before venturing
back out into the lonely cold or onto the dangerous
roads where they all continue doing the things
I can no longer do, drawing deep breaths of fresh air,
tasting the earth's bounty, loving one another
despite the relatively low return on such a dubious
investment . . . all part of the spirit's long parade of souls
who adopt organic form and do the best they can.

ON THE PARADE ROUTE

Some days you are that proud fellow
out front of the marching band,
holding the heavy golden mace,
setting the pace for everyone.

Some days you are the poor fool
following the horse brigade with
a flathead shovel, scooping
the steaming odorous piles.

But let's face it, most days you are
merely the third clarinet from the left,
trying to keep step with the others,
hoping for enough spit to wet your reed.

MAN BENEATH A TREE

A Spotted Towhee sings in the Magnolia.
Her quavering trills rise to fill the air, then
fall into stillness. On my mind this morning—
meetings and appointments. Yet I find myself

reveling in the bird's alternating melody.
I catch myself breathing in sync with
her rhythm. How easy it would be to drop my
cares and surrender my body to the lush grass!

On this very day my soul might finally blossom,
like the large, soft, vanilla-scented tepals
in the branches overhead. In the shade of this tree,
I might receive the secret bliss that awaits us all.

The Magnolia is easy to love; so too the Towhee,
whose tattered refrain has awakened this sacred
yearning. But I fear it may yield to the noise
of duties and obligations that also beckon.

Standing in the sanctuary of the moment, will I
give myself into the keeping of her gentle song,
or turn a deaf ear to love's intervention, her
mundane and ubiquitous song of deliverance?

THE WIDOW IN SPRINGTIME

A robin stops singing and sounds the alarm—
the red shouldered hawk returns to her nest
high in the crooked Monterey Pine. Two chicks
pop fuzzy heads above the rim to receive her prey.

It is a bright morning in late April. On her patio
beneath the pine, a woman wraps herself
in a shawl, stretches out on her chaise lounge
and sips a blue cocktail through a pink straw.

She will not raise her sunglasses to rest atop
her head. She will not fill in the official forms.
What she needs is a cup of strong black coffee.
But need has been eaten this morning by want.

It is undoubtedly the season of resurrection.
Who among us will take up the robin's song?

NOT A POEM FOR CHILDREN

The big red fire engine moaned and groaned
up and down the suburban streets, grinding
from gear to gear, the men in red metal hats
with huge wrenches opening the giant release
valves on the yellow hydrants. Children squealed

as the water gushed into the street, raising
a torrent of hilarity. They splashed
and yelped at the miracle of fast-flowing,
cool water on a hot, hot summer's day.
Refreshed, one little boy ran after the fire truck,

first thinking, then hoping, and finally believing
that he could catch the truck as it barreled on up
the street, around the corner, and onto the next street.
He ran and ran, the great silver bumper just beyond
his reach. He could dive and grab for it,

as his legs pumped and his chest heaved,
he could dive and grab and pull himself up—
like Batman up the side of a building or Roy Rogers
from one horse's back to another. It could be done.
He ran, and as he ran he pictured himself

diving and grabbing and pulling himself to stand
on the rear bumper; he imagined the jubilation
of the whole neighborhood as he stood and waved
to the passing houses from the rear of the big
red truck! But his legs and his lungs grew tired;

the truck groaned and pulled away, away. At last
the boy slowed, stopped, and stood . . . drenched,
wheezing, alone in the middle of the sweltering
July Saturday, heat waves rising from the asphalt,
the truck belching and moaning its way out of sight.

THREE

100,000 ITEMS TO BE FOUND
INSIDE BUDDHA'S GREAT BELLY

10,000 dark clouds of plague that
   envelope the guilty and the innocent.
Petals of 10,000 red-orange poppies
   picked from coastal California cliffs.

Groans and wails of 10,000 suffering beings
   now and throughout all time.
10,000 temple bells resounding across
   the bright meadows of the world.

10,000 cups of bitter yellow bile
   steeped in our resentment and desire.
10,000 powdery white cloud cakes
   with creamy luscious centers.

Thorns from 10,000 wild brambles
   that deftly separate sinew from skin.
Downy feathers of 10,000 geese flying
   across deep shadows of the moon.

The stench of 10,000 corpses as they rot
   and decay and grandly decompose.
Clean breezes drawn across 10,000
   rain-soaked mountain ferns in heaven.

APRIL 11, 1954

Let us remember and revere this date,
recorded as the least interesting day
in human history. On a planet ravaged
at an ever-increasing rate by our race
of brutal bipedal savages, on this day
damage was mitigated by a preponderance
of inaction. People awoke and mouthed
their milk toast, their cold cuts, and their
leftover meatloaf. They sang "Swinging
on a Star" in the shower. They wore
their poodle skirts and rolled up sleeves with
little starch and shoes that didn't pinch.
No revolutions began on this day.
Not one person sank into a funk of regret.
No one important was born; no one famous died.
Everything remained on an even keel.
Nothing remarkable happened at all.

Let us indeed remember and revere that
gloriously uneventful day of April 11, 1954.
With no escalation of geopolitical tensions,
President Eisenhower was content to slice
his drives into the drink. Senator McCarthy
drank himself into an early, harmless stupor.
Some teenagers kissed under elm trees.
Children lolled on swing sets in the park.
A high school Algebra teacher sat at a red light
dreaming up problems for the next exam.
A farmer raised the bill of his cap and hailed

a stream of puffy white cumulus. A secretary
stopped typing a letter to wind her watch.
A New Jersey pediatrician scribbled a poem
on his prescription pad. May we be given more
such days in which the devil dozes in the straw,
and nothing really remarkable happens at all.

IN LINE AT STARBUCKS

Through the speakers Norah Jones croons
"Come Away with Me" as though she really
means it. Our line isn't budging. We shuffle
our feet and check our phones. In the news
this morning, the president has deigned
to make us great by serving himself first.
The crumbs that fall from his table, those
are for us. He has cheated more people than
most of us will ever meet. The couple behind me
in line for coffee cradles their newborn,
fussing over the diaper bag—did they
remember to pack the wipes? Someone mutters,
"What a world to bring a child into."
The young parents either don't hear or choose
to ignore him. The wisdom of youth, such as it is,
may lay in such selective attention.
After all, there must be a million reasons
not to procreate. We each take a step forward
in line. The baby coos and wriggles.
"What'll you have?" asks the barista.
"Dark stuff," I reply, "but let's add sweetener."
"Real or fake?" she asks. Good question.
Do I risk diabetes from the real sugar
or cancer from the fake stuff? I figure I have
a few more years before tumors and tremors.
I think, in fact, there are at least a million
good reasons not to procreate. None can
stand up to Norah Jones' breathy refrain.

WE'LL TAKE A CUP OF KINDNESS YET

It's the week between Christmas and New Year's.
Starbucks is more crowded than usual.
COVID is spiking, as is Influenza and RSV—
a *tripledemic* say the news sources.
But hardly anyone is masked. Most Americans,
it seems, have decided to roll the dice
with their immune systems this winter.

There are two women at the table next to me
and one of them has been talking non-stop
since I sat down. Every thought in her head
spews out at the friend who sits across from her—
a friend who has not got a word in edgewise.

I don't know how the woman continues to breathe
since she hasn't paused, not visibly, to inhale.
She has somehow developed the technique
of the famous Tibetan throat-singers; however,
her words are not guttural Buddhist blessings, just
mind-numbing dribble about her astonishingly boring life.

I begin by pitying the stalwart friend, clearly
a hostage to this woman's rampaging ego.
For just such a situation was the old finger-gun
to the temple invented. Then I stop feeling sorry
for her; she's not a saint, only a fool who suffers fools.

I realize I'm really reacting to the cosmic trap
we're all caught in, for the woman's verbal diarrhea
is merely the issue of a cluttered brain and a vacant soul.
O Lord, how pitiful is humanity, me most of all,
because all I can think to do with myself today is to
sit next to this calamity and scribble in my notebook.

Finally, the friend suggests that since
the rain has paused, they might now perhaps
continue their walk. Incredibly, the woman
hears this interjection and agrees. They stand, she
of course babbling all the way to the thank God Almighty
door, and, mercifully, just like that, they are gone.

It's quiet, or relatively so, until I hear the man
two tables over, lecturing his laptop; add to
that the loud-talking shift supervisor reciting
a litany of training details to a young apprentice;
add to that the crappy music coming through
the speakers—that awful synthetic beat that
makes the blood pumping from my heart want to
reverse course and go back inside to hide.

Of course, I could leave myself, just get up and go—
but to where? For Starbucks is only a representative
sampling of the wide world, and these incredibly boring
self-obsessed people are, in fact, my people,

yes, and here we all are, Virgil at our elbow and the angels
on vacation in Las Vegas, the thumping of our desperate
hearts down here in the seventh circle, partakers all in . . .
what . . . a hopeless procession down hell's Main Street?

No wonder I've been having panic attacks.
Soon enough the mindless chatter blends into a kind
of cooing sound. God, or someone, switches
the music channel to Miles Davis' "So What."
His long soaring trumpet solo soothes my spirit.
A compassionate barista brings me a free refill and
a sample of day-old pastries. I take a moment
to look around the room, which appears less crowded
now; the yellow LEDs have taken on a milder glow,
and the battlefield has turned back to meadow.

It's an ordinary rainy day during the week between
Christmas and New Year's (a newborn refugee
among astonished farmhands on one side,
and a worldwide street party on the other).
How is it that this soft-hearted comedy so often
plays as pure tragedy in our beleaguered brains?
And why is it that I keep forgetting to remember
that someone other than you or me abides
within and without all the noise of the world,
God, or some other lonesome caretaker of our misery
who sadly takes, sadly takes and gladly gives.

MUSIC THROUGH THE SPEAKERS

The young baristas at Starbucks like the frenetic
kitsch of 1970s disco on busy mornings,
a rhythmical partner between them and their
machinery in the daily dance of woosh
and splash, hiss and drip, the chanting of
customer names and the vaguely Italianate
titles of drinks—hot, warm, cool, and cold.
My own preference from my comfy leather seat
near the window runs to smooth jazz or the mild
twang of folky guitar riffs accompanied by
sincere lyrics of the unrequited and misunderstood.
How surprised we all were to hear the sudden
drawl of Willie Nelson break through from
Planet Austin, where he orbits as the god of western
swing, he the long-eared, wrinkled, and
bemused crooner of the cannabis-cowboy set,
he of the Aquarian Age golf ball-whacking,
splintery hole in the Martin N-20 plucker of very
damn Texas but somehow universal nylon strings,
he who named his guitar after Roy Rogers'
beautiful Palomino stallion, whom Roy outfitted
with a gold and silver saddle that they wore
in numerous parades, Rose and otherwise,
(in fact, he and Dale waved to me sitting
lonesome in a lawn chair near the corner
of Orange Grove and Colorado Boulevards
during the original Age of Disco) when the cartoonish
fringe of their costumes seemed like a beautiful relic
from the Jurassic Age, and I, who had my first

Willie Nelson album at home on the stereo,
worked to memorize "Love is like a dying ember /
And only memories remain / And through the ages
I'll remember / Blue eyes cryin' in the rain."

AFTERMATH

So many things went wrong so fast.
When hope slipped out the back door,
our silver set tucked in his black kit bag,
we took up smoking; we drank too much,
much more than we should. Why not?

Then one night the rich tang of skunk
wafted through the bedroom window,
filling our house with wild nature,
reminding us how fragile these glue
and paper walls, how thin our pale skin.

Could we live again as all once lived—
exposed to storm, thief, quake, killer?
This morning we hear hope's steps
on the back stoop; he is hungry, having
eaten what food our silver could buy.

Light and warmth flood the window.
The sun moves again among the clouds.
The soil yet breathes its tender breaths.
We stretch and reach and walk once more
among our haggard, shell-shocked clan.

So many things went wrong so fast.
Darkness, we thought, would last and last.
With morning the hummingbird returns
to the honeysuckle—her green quivering flank,
her long nose sunk deep in pink.

ABRAHAM PREPARING TO SACRIFICE HIS SON

—on a painting by Marc Chagall

Although Isaac is laid bare upon the stone altar,
Abraham's knife is turned heavenward, as if
threatening the impassive angel hovering in the sky.
The curve of the angel's lip suggests he has just
declared clemency. Isaac couldn't care less, having
prepared himself for the worst. It's Abraham
whose face registers relief. The medieval rabbis knew
what women everywhere know, that while the men
play out their little dramas of heaven and earth,
it's those left out of the official portrait that make
the real sacrifices. The rabbis speculate that Sarah's
death in the very next chapter is precipitated
by a broken heart, having watched her old fool pack up
the asses, tie her beloved boy to the saddle,
tuck his best knife into his belt, and light out
for the distant mountain of blood and fire and smoke.

THE ROOSTER

—on a painting by Marc Chagall

In the foreground rides a woman
on the neck of a giant rooster:
see the angle of her hips as
she straddles him, the glad way
he receives her heft; see her
tender embrace, her rosy cheek
upon his clownish head. Behold
the stupid grin upon his silly beak.
Preen your feathers while ye may,
young lovers—the shimmering world
will not forever sparkle so.

In the background a couple cuddle
in a tiny rowboat afloat upon
a dappled sea of ethereal blue-green—
eerie and lovely as love itself.
Small boat, big sea: adrift we all shall be:
oh, cling to me, cling to me, cling—
(hear the minor key of heavenly spheres,
hear the swirling planets breaking free)
cling, and do not let me be, for
the boat, brothers and sisters, is tiny indeed
and the sea, the blue-green sea . . . immense.

PRIMARY COLORS

I

A couple stroll arm in arm through a field
so flush with yellow daffodils it would make
Wordsworth fart with envy. They aren't wandering
lonely as a cloud; they have each other . . . so,
by the way, did Wordsworth, who conveniently
edited his sister Dorothy out of his famous poem,
which is his right, of course—as an autonomous artist
he may add or subtract as he wishes; even so,
there are those who notice that Dorothy's journal,
dated two years before the poem's publication,
contains that elegant description of daffodil heaven—
so, apparently, he was not only not wandering
lonely as a cloud, but he did not actually
capture the scene until he copied it from his sister
and then represented it as his own, making him a thief,
a liar, and kind of a dick. But he's not the first
self-aggrandizing artist, is he? Nor will he be the last.
And not the first man to exploit the talent
of a smarter woman and take credit for her work.
Surely he will not be the last. But what of
that couple I mentioned strolling through the field?
I'm not sure why I mentioned them. They just
happened to appear, and I decided not to edit them out.
It's the sky above them that matters most—
the jocund, cloudless, impossibly blue sky.

II

Wikipedia tells us that "the eye perceives blue
when observing light with a dominant wavelength
between approximately 450 and 495 nanometers,"
which helps us not at all. Surveys show
blue is commonly associated with harmony,
faithfulness, confidence, the imagination, and
sometimes sadness. This, too, helps us not at all.
In the wake of his friend Casagemas' suicide,
Picasso turned blue for almost four years.
He wandered the streets of Paris without
a winter coat and without a lick of sense.
The rose period that followed bubbled up
from the steamy geyser inside Picasso's blue brain;
it clung to the rooftops of the city long after he,
heron-like, migrated south, following Matisse on a
wavelength that reaches approximately 700 nanometers,
which perhaps helps us a little. If only a little.

III

Robert Burns is the Scotsman who compared
love to a red, red rose, which blooms into a thing
of delicate beauty, then rots—so it is, the simile
would suggest, with love. We might also conclude
that love, before it rots, fills our nostrils with sweetness,
and that love, if we're not careful, may shred us

with its thorns. But most of all love is red.
And not just red but red red. Like the matador's cape,
like the sun burning through dense smoke, like
the Technicolor splash that animates Hitchcock's *Vertigo*
to the rhythm of Bernard Hermann's dizzying castanets.
But it's the green in that movie (and at the opposite end
of the color wheel) that, like mint, settles us
when we begin to spin, and the green that saturates
the screen in Del Toro's *The Shape of Water*, and that
seduces us with its vaguely evolutionary glow . . .
from green water we came, to green water we will return.
And so sinks Robbie Burns, even *his* best-laid schemes
long ago gang agley, and so he slowly sinks into the waters
of that lonely green green Scottish loch, with only
the flotsam of his songs floating around his tousled head.

ANGEL OF THE WATERS

Bathed in October sunlight, her feet appear first,
at the end of the pedestrian tunnel, in the center
of Central Park, hovering above Bethesda Fountain.

Next, the iron robes flowing down her body—
a progressive revelation: the knees of iron,
the iron hips and iron shoulders, the delicate iron
arms, outstretched, reaching toward the saved
and the damned. Finally, her stern countenance.

When he exits the tunnel she floats there in full
splendor, and there, overhead, the iron wingspan,
upraised in feathery cruelty. Will she lift him
by the scruff, hoist him above grime, mold, misery,
or will she trample him beneath her naked iron feet?

Is this the way memory works—does it gather
from bottom to top, loom and hover forever?
When the mother chose to disbelieve her boy before
he had a chance to speak, he knew he had been tricked
by one experienced in deceit, by one who knew
how to trigger a mother's fury against a child
whom instinct had otherwise taught her to protect,
by one who schemed against him even as she pinned
him to the bathroom floor and ground her hips
until the cold tiles imprinted themselves on his back.

The art of conjuring such darkness was deep mystery
to him then. Now, as the lift and thrust of an iron angel's
wings heals all but the lingering pain of a mother's
unwitting betrayal, let the paralytic enter the pool
at last, and let the murky waters finally be disturbed.

LET OUR TEARS BE FOR RAIN

Strong men have begun to gather in packs,
conspiring against the dawn. They want
to see us crack and bleed. They want to drum
the rhythm of the tide as it sweeps

against heaps of fly infested kelp. Some
of us have developed an ache deep
in our bones, beyond the reach of healing
hands or soothing balms. Some have begun

to weep beyond control. In this, the season
of our parching, let our tears be for rain.
Keep us, O Lord, from grasping at air
as the drowning do. Let us rather aspire

as the meek ever do, to inhale hope, and exhale
love so buoyant that it lifts us above this tide.

EASTERTIDE

Each April a row of cherry trees
blooms along this winding path.

Girls of the neighborhood appear
in spring dresses, twirling parasols.

By May the delicate blossoms
fall at our restless feet;

pink snowflakes sweep in windy
swirls, then settle afresh.

Gardeners arrive with blowers
and burlap bags. Our moment

of renewal becomes a matter
of memory, meant to carry us

through the hot dry days ahead,
not to mention the long dark

evenings of dank imaginings,
hunger pangs, lovers who lay dying.

AUBADE

Around the perimeter of our back patio
I've placed solar lights. All day long
the tiny photovoltaic cells collect
and store the sun's energy. At odd times
during the lonely night, I awaken and
look out the window at gently
gleaming bits of sunlight casting shadows
around the yard. In the glow I can just
make out the shapes of flowers bowing
in their pots, and the grain of graying
redwood in the panels of our back fence.
By morning the sun itself awakens
every living thing in my sight with color,
color that dazzles and pacifies. Stirring
the birds from their nests, the sun
prompts a morning symphony of gratitude.
Never in my lifetime has the sun failed
to perform this tender mercy. Long before
I called myself I, the sun garnered my praise.
Long after this I disappears into the earth
the birds will sing their poems in my place.
Until then, let this small singing of mine
join the welcoming choir of each day's dawning.

SOMETIMES IT WORKS

For a dog, the standard training command
is "leave it." Often the command is accompanied
by a treat; ideally, no treat is needed.
The success of "leave it" depends on many
things—the trigger, the time of day, hours
since the last meal, the proper alignment
of certain auspicious stars and planets.

If my dog Ginny and I pass a bunny
or a duck, usually "leave it" works. But if
a squirrel twitches into sudden motion,
on the ground, up a trunk, across a branch or,
god forbid, along a fence top, her muscles
tense, her fur stands at attention, her
adrenal glands hastily lock and load.

No treat can pull her back from this brink.
My squirrels also take me by seeming surprise—
random fears, dark imaginings, or historical
re-runs. So deep the instinct to fight or flee.
So quick the lit fuse sizzles along the spine.
Only the measured breath can release me,
the prayer beads through the fingers,
the steady mantra on the lips—my treat.

LET THERE BE PEACE IN THE VALLEY

Up against the foothills of a valley
once named for Saint Clare of Assisi,
Ginny and I sit in the shade beneath
a redwood. The grass is lush here,
and the tree guards us from the worst
heat of midday. It is a busy corner.
Across the street is a church
with a large cross atop its steeple,
a familiar site in the suburbs of
North America, though less and less.

According to the ancient story, general
Constantine's dream-vision of a cross
upon the sun, captioned with the words
"By this sign, conquer," inspired his victory
at the Battle of Milvian Bridge,
securing him the power to transform
a modest peace-loving religious cult
into a world-devouring warrior's code,
the irony of which was completely lost
on the famously dim-witted emperor.

Conquering foes and enslaving them
then pillaging and defiling the planet
while claiming God's ultimate blessing
may not hold the appeal it once did.
Ginny and I show little ambition.

In the tranquil shade of this redwood
let our silent vigil be our protest
against all such shenanigans. Grass on this
corner is lush, and the tree guards us
just fine from the heat of the midday sun.

FOUR

HAT TRICK

Tired of playing it safe and sane,
I've recently traded my poet's head
for a hockey head. All I ever did
with my poet's head was feed it
veggies and fish oil and walk it
through the woods on manicured
trails. What a dull head it was
all those dreary suburban years.
Now I've got a wild old noggin
that's been used and abused by
flying pucks and high-swung sticks
and the insults of brutally honest
hockey hooligans. This head has drunk
gallons of cheap vodka and devoured
ribs and hot dogs, spat chew and curses
through its busted chicklets and shaggy
red whiskers. This hockey head has
never voted, never read James Joyce,
never shopped at Nordstrom's
for a pair of socks to match its new tie.

This hockey head is not about to add
its name to a petition to protect
the rare spotted butterflies of Borneo
or sip vintage Chardonnay in a mahogany-
paneled Napa tasting room. Thank God
this hockey head will never sit in a pew
and sing "For the Beauty of the Earth."

Come Saturday night, I fully expect it
to be my ticket to the drunk tank.
No doubt three different women
will slap this hockey head, their husbands
will want to punch this crooked hockey nose
on this splotchy hockey mug.
These green hockey eyes will both
be blackened before long. This head
may even deliver me into the hands
of vengeful bookies who will collect its debts
with lead pipes and zip guns.

By trading my poet's head for this
hockey head, I've just walked my chubby,
pale body into a world of pain and indignity.
I've gone and put myself into the path
of a runaway Zamboni in flames.
Don't you dare look at me with that
disapproving glare. Bring your accountant head
over here, you smug provincial hoser.
I'm going to smack that successful grin
off your spa-conditioned skin.
I'm about to beat you the way
grandma does an old throw rug.
My new hockey brain just fired
a clapper of testosterone into
my bloodstream, and these flabby old
biceps are just twitching with hockey vigor.

A PART OF THE MAIN

My enlarged prostate is strangling
my urethra the way Boris Karloff
strangles Ernest Thesiger in *The Ghoul*.

In the middle of the night, I can't
even make it to the toilet.
I fill empty mason jars that

I leave on the bedside table.
One day I trapped an ordinary
house spider in one of the jars,

filled it with pee during the night,
awoke at dawn to find the spider
floating in amber like that astronaut

in *2001* who got locked out
of the capsule and drifted,
arms and legs akimbo, into space.

On the island of Kauai I was
confronted by a huge cane spider
on the stucco wall of a rented condo.

I couldn't bring myself to kill it
because the intricate design on its back
resembled the swirling island designs

tattooed around the muscular arms
of Poipu surfers. The spider
seemed to belong there more than I.

Once on an island off the coast
of Belize, I came back from the beach
to find a black jungle spider

the size of my palm on the door
to the bathroom. I really had to pee.
So I smacked it to the ground

with my snorkel mask and crushed it
with my rubber fins. The Rorschach's
design its guts made on the floor tiles

looked like gun moll Gloria Grahame's
face after Lee Marvin threw
a pot of hot coffee at her

in *The Big Heat*, the same movie
in which Glenn Ford's wife and daughter
get blown up in a car bomb

meant for him because Ford was getting
too close to cracking an extortion racket.
Where did Glenn Ford belong?

He quit the force in anger, so
he wasn't a cop anymore, yet
he still staked out the gangsters

like a trapdoor spider who waits
for the right moment to spring
from the ground and devour his prey,

which reminds anyone who's seen it
of that demented preacher Robert Mitchum
played in *Night of the Hunter*, where he

stalks the children of his nemesis,
love and hate tattooed on alternate knuckles,
serenading them with a creepy hymn

that no one can sing to God anymore
without thinking of Mitchum's satanic
hyper-calm glare. Mitchum did it

because he didn't belong anywhere
but prison and, like Charlie Manson,
he would do anything to get back in.

It's not pee but a glass of plain water
that the child in *Signs* leaves around
the house and that turned out to be

the only way to kill the spider-like
aliens that invaded her father's cornfields.
It's hard to watch that movie now

because it stars that alleged anti-Semite
Mel Gibson who doesn't really belong
among the liberal Hollywood elites

such as Tom Hanks, who played a Fed Ex
executive that gets stranded on an
uncharted island in the middle of the Pacific.

Tom Hanks certainly doesn't belong
on that island, but just where
does he belong?—in *Catch Me If You Can*,

perhaps, where he plays the clever G-man
who pursues the spidery Leo DiCaprio.
Hanks, a diabetic, probably has an enlarged

prostate, too, which is strangling
his urethra in the worst way.
Sometime soon he may find himself

awake in the middle of the night
wishing he had a jar to pee in
because he's not going to make it

to the toilet, which is where pee belongs.
All of this to say that (much as I hate
to admit it) John Donne was probably

right when he said no man is an island
because each of us belong to one
another whether we like it or not,

including spiders and enlarged glands
and demented preachers and the numerous
islands that presume to separate us.

YUCK

About my annual prostate exam, my doctor feels
the same way I do about grading papers: it's not
our favorite part of the job, but it has to be done.
As I drop my shorts and place my elbows on
the exam table, he snaps the blue latex glove
into place and readies the tube of lubricant.

For me, this routine is briefly uncomfortable
and mildly humiliating; from his angle, it must be
downright disgusting. Yet he's careful to stick
to medical protocol: he tosses the spent glove
into the waste bin and makes his overly-polite exit
from the exam room, as his oxford heels click a hasty
retreat down the hall to his lavender-scented office.

Well, too bad. I once graded thirty, count 'em thirty,
boldly plagiarized, barely literate research papers
in a single sitting. I, too, had to hold my virtual nose
at the stench and adjourn to the local tavern for
a medicinal pint of Guinness and a big-screen display
of ritualized violence just to scrub my mind clear.

Handing the papers back to their authors, I also
found it hard to hide my revulsion. But we must
not allow the masks of our respective roles to slip
from the sweaty rim of our faces. Ah, humanity!—
often does the issue of your body and your mind
require an ironclad stomach, a sanitary glove,
and a sweet-smelling strategy for escape.

OUT-PATIENT PROCEDURE

The surgeon removed my stone-laden gall bladder
and took it out for a walk. He leashed it up
and strolled around the hospital grounds.

At first it plodded and waddled and whimpered.
Soon it squatted next to each clump of bushes
to do its business—one stone at a time to begin

and then in clusters. Its pace quickened. Before long
it trotted at the surgeon's heel, tongue lolling,
squirting bile through its duct like a pink bota.

In the recovery room, I lay on a sterile gurney
dreaming myself down a milkshake river toward
cheeseburger oblivion. By the time I awoke,

the surgeon and my gall bladder were on a flight
to Wyoming, where no one goes without a damn
good reason. Come spring my gall bladder will

flush quail for its new master . . . and all around
the hospital grounds will sprout yellow gall flowers
with sweaty perfumed layers of feathery petals.

HELLO DARKNESS

Here we go round again, my old friend,
dancing our slow and dismal dance.
I hoped that you had gone for good,
taken your minor key from my door,
shuffled on to some other house.

Instead you paused in the vestibule,
waiting there, ear cocked, listening
for sounds of sweetness and light,
waiting until you might noiselessly
return, slip your arm around my waist

and take me in a gentle whirl,
smooth at first, an easy turn, and
then insert your rough right hand into
my soft left, curling your fingers
into a lock, your polished shoes

scuffing my polished floor. Somewhat
dizzied by your command, without
much struggle, I am swept again
into your trance. There—see that trace
of light around the window's shade,

hear the cheery jangles in the street below?
Such light and joy are worlds away.
For now, there is only you and me
dancing our slow and dismal dance,
going round again, my old, old friend.

THE BEST THING TO DO

Sexton poured herself a vodka and donned her
mother's fur coat before closing the garage door
and starting the motor of her favorite car.
Different house, similar neighborhood: Plath
lay her head in the gas oven, the children
safely sealed in their room, towel beneath the door.

Berryman jumped from a bridge. Crane leapt
from the steamship SS Orizaba. Seneca had to struggle
across the Styx: when his body failed to bleed out,
he ingested poison, which didn't work, so he climbed
into a hot bath and suffocated from the steam.
Mishima committed seppuku, method of the samurai.

Teasdale swallowed more pills than she could count.
Lugones mixed himself a fascist cocktail of cyanide
and whiskey. Having survived Auschwitz, Borowski
gassed himself. Lindsay drank a bottle of lye. Yesenin
hanged himself. Mayakovsky shot himself as only a poet
would: not through the head but through his Bolshevik heart.

She wasn't known for her poetry, but Woolf's method
still prompts admiration: after filling the pockets
of her overcoat with stones, she walked into
the river Ouse. The note she left Leonard said,
"I feel certain that I am going mad again . . .
I am doing what seems the best thing to do."

CARPE, FOOL

Nothing happened today. That's not true.
Not exactly true. Today was not momentous.
The direction of my life wasn't changed today.

That was yesterday. Yesterday everything
changed. In fact, my life came to a screeching halt.
You might say it pivoted in a new direction.

So far as I know, yesterday was the most
significant day of my life. Or second most.
But not today. Today is, as the saying goes,

just another day. Except for one thing.
I died yesterday. So today, as it turns out,
is the first day in what I presume to be an endless

string of days of me being dead. And, really,
not much happens when you're dead.
In case you were wondering, nothing

is what happens when you're dead.
So live, you stupid son of a bitch.
Stop reading this. Do what I tell you.

Put this aside. It's not important.
Drink a cold bottle of beer. Go out
your front door and embrace a stranger.

Plant a wet kiss on the mailman.
While I'm busy being dead, you should
get busy living. Even a little living is enough.

Too soon you'll join me in this business
of being dead, and all of your poems will
begin and end with "nothing happened today."

DOWNPOUR

They were two tourists in the little village of Boppard
on the Rhine. They had arrived by train from Cologne,
having admired the cathedral the Allied bombers had spared,
having gawked at the three medieval relics upon its altar—
the Magi's caskets of Gold, Frankincense, and Myrrh.

They had eaten a plate of cheese and sausages, sipped
two glasses of the local Riesling, and now they were
strolling along the river in their travel khakis and
cotton shirts. Tipsy, they thought the boardwalk quaint
and followed its serpentine path along the shore.
Had they even noticed the dark clouds moving in
or the choppy current of the great river roiling past?

They'd gone about a mile when the clouds opened
and the thunder rumbled. They ran for cover, settling
on a bench beneath an enormous oak. The Germans
strolled by under umbrellas; they were used to fast-moving
summer storms and the sight of soaked and shivering
Americans clinging to each other under their trees.

Bolts broke over the hilltops; crackling echoes filled
the valley. Barges chugged against the current.
White-tailed eagles criss-crossed beneath the sparking
clouds, and huge raindrops tumbled into the river.

Traveling light, they hadn't followed any star;
they hadn't lugged any gifts for any new king, nor
regarded the passing of one era into another.

They indeed were ignorant of the sky, and
no one along these banks thought them wise.

Back at the hotel that evening, clothes hang-drying
in the shower, they sat on the balcony as
the barometer dropped, reading the history
of castles on the opposite shore. They propped
their bare feet on the railing and, like two invincible
lovers in the marble tower of an ancient myth,
never considered that they might soon be
swept away by forces beyond their reckoning.

BITTER CROP

Two long rows of poplars
line the gravel avenue
between barracks in Dachau.

Down the avenue march the guards
and the prisoners, the whores and the SS.
All flourish in the lush Bavarian soil.

All measure with lengthening shadows
the long days spent assembling Death's
bright and blunt appliances.

Eighty-five years later, gone are the barracks,
the guards and the prisoners, the whores
and the SS. The poplars yet stand,

shading tourists who snack and stare
at photos of American GIs not long
off the farm as they bare everlasting witness

to the disease we carry in our skulls.
At the very end of the long, empty avenue
you may light a candle and confess your part.

OCCURRENCE ON BUBB ROAD

Last summer a man was found floating face down
in the percolation pond. He had drained a bottle
of vodka, filled his pockets with rocks, and walked
into the tepid water until his lungs went soggy.

When the sheriff removed the yellow crime scene
tape from around the tree trunks, the children
could once again take the short cut trail to the 7-11.
Let not the path of commerce be blocked,
neither by procedure nor by pity.

This summer I float on an inflated rubber duck
in my neighbor's swimming pool on the hottest
afternoon of the year. The smoke rises from his
absurd barbeque, sends signals to hikers
in the foothills that we come in peace,
we suburban loafers of the flatlands.

Hey, you know what? my neighbor says,
apropos of nothing. That floater
in the percolation pond was my wife's first
husband. He never did recover from the war
in Afghanistan. Is that why he did it? I ask.
Did what? my neighbor says. Oh, that. No,
well yes. She says he came home a haunted man.
I can imagine, I say. I can't, he says.

When he flips the steaks, the grill sizzles
with pleasure, as the fat carries on a conversation
with the red-hot coals. I paddle the duck
in a circle, one hand pushing the water one way,
the other hand pulling in the other.
And the sun dares the clouds to come near—
the white-hot sun in the terribly blue sky.

FLAMES

The town of Paradise, California
burns into deep autumn.
Smoke and ash, smoke and ash—
cinders fall upon San Francisco.

Jimi Hendrix's Stratocaster
burns on stage in Monterey,
the stoned audience mesmerized
by his conjuring hands.

Nero makes human torches
of Christians who refuse allegiance.
Buddhist monks kneel in the streets
of Saigon, burning.

And you, Norman Morrison, burn
beneath Robert McNamara's office window.
In the arms of a bystander,
your baby reeks of kerosene.

RECLUSE

They had startled me all summer long—in the corner
of the shower, my sock drawer, the mailbox—
with their spiny legs and violins on their brown bellies.
Too messy to squash, I trapped them in jars
and left them to suffocate. My Jainist friend, Darshika,
tells me there's no difference between killing a spider
and killing a human. Killing is killing, she says.

I reply, But I don't want to live in a spider cave.

Yes but, Darshika says, you don't appreciate
the karmic imbalance caused by your bloodlust.
Her face registering disgust, she asks, What sort of
animal are you?
       A human animal, I reply.
And we are killers, big time. Wherever you look,
you see humans engaged in the fine art of killing.
Besides, I tell my Jainist friend, I don't see a lot
of striving for enlightenment. Most humans seem content
with chocolates and television. Really, I say,
and this is no joke, I am going to go on killing spiders
if they are in my house. But maybe you might say
some prayers for me, that I may be spared this indignity.

Why not just release them? she asks. Set them free
from the jars in the park down near the creek,
where they might thrive.
      You still don't understand, I say.

I don't want them to thrive. I want them to die,
and I want you to stop judging me.

                                        You want your cake
and to eat it too.

                            Of course, I say. Have you got any cake?
I'd like creamy rich deep dark chocolate with fudge
frosting please.

                        How cavalier you are with the lives
of creatures who share the planet with us.

                                            Not only that,
I say, now I'm committing the sin of gluttony in my heart.
I won't be able to rest until I have some chocolate cake.

Come downtown with me, she says. We will stop
at the vegan bakery, and I will buy you some cake.

You love me anyway, don't you? I ask. You love me
even though I wreak havoc with the karmic balance.

Sort of, she replies. What I'm also doing is preventing you
from eating cake made with eggs from the non-vegan bakery.

Bless your missionary heart, I say, stepping over the beetle
crossing the sidewalk ahead of me.

                            Later, sated with cake and tea,
I turn back on my own to find that beetle—and crush him
underfoot.

TRANSFIGURATIONS

There was a man who found himself drawn into
a large holly oak along a suburban parkway.
He stood admiring the tree one day while his dog
squatted and peed near the trunk. Then he hugged
the tree, tenderly at first, as if it were a frail elderly
friend. He hugged the tree closer, tighter, with his
whole being. He pressed his cheek against the
dappled bark. His dog began to whimper and circle
the tree. She pulled her leash from the man's loosening
fingers. She licked the man's bare leg. She tugged
with her teeth at the hem of his shorts. She barked
once, took a step back, and barked again.

The oak returned the man's embrace by welcoming him
inside. His body melded with the tree. Soon only
his sky-blue Aloha shirt and khaki shorts hung upon
the bark. And then the shirt and the shorts slipped
to the ground. The man's dog wandered a few steps away,
then returned to sniff his clothing. Eventually the dog
continued her walk, dragging her leash on down the street.

As the man's cells were absorbed into the texture
of the wood, his skin and sinews and bones and blood
all joined the inner circles of the trunk, grew skyward
into the tree's branches and twigs, leaves and acorns.
Was there anything resembling a man inside that oak
by winter, when the cold winds shook the branches
and chilled the roots, as the rains beat against
what had once been his drowsy and bedraggled heart?

The dog grew to love another master. The two
visit the tree often. On occasion the dog's new human
rubs his fingers along the seams of the tree.
He shields his eyes and looks up at the squirrels.
He listens to the songbirds, who sing with greater
vigor than in any other neighborhood tree.
He pats the tree and moves on down the street.

People disappear from our sight each year. Children.
Old people. Even those with babies to raise and
careers in full steam. We imagine kidnappers,
serial killers, jealous lovers on a spree. How many
rather sink into creeks, joining the current
as it flows to bay, inlet, or ocean, swimming into
another life? How many take to the sky with bright wings,
gliding thermals along seaside cliffs? How many indeed
burrow into the mud or slither under roots and rocks,
becoming one with layers of sediment? You yourself
may one day find that you prefer to exist only
in the woeful song of the black-headed grosbeak.

FIVE

AMERICAN FEMME FATALE

Like Barbara Stanwyck in *Double Indemnity*,
she spots our naiveté beneath the fakery
of our fedora hat and blue woolen suit,
our salesman's grin and impish demeanor.

She smells our desperation when we lean in
to inhale her perfume. She cracks wise
and turns an aloof shoulder, then winks.
Or so we think. Was that a wink?

She plays us like a trout lured into the shallows—
just for kicks at first, but later she fries us
in a pan with lemon and butter, dash of salt,
dash of pepper, splash of whiskey. Down

her long, elegant gullet we go, sweet Jesus,
like the lump of a rat down the cool length
of a shiny black garden snake, who slithers
on back to the shade of the gnarled old tree

whose strange fruit droops into the shadows,
whose fruit hangs low, real low down,
whose misshapen bittersweet fruit resembles
the jackboot, the cudgel, the noose.

WAS YOU EVER BIT BY A DEAD BEE?

Bogie is sitting in a smoky bar in a colonial Caribbean
outpost filled with Warner Brothers' tropical props—
all the usual palm fronds and political menace.

Hoagie Carmichael is noodling at the piano.
Lauren Bacall is hustling a rich American out
of his wallet. Of course there are Nazis afoot.

People from the underground resistance keep asking
Bogie to help. He's got a boat. He knows the waters.
He's sympathetic. But he sticks his neck out for nobody.

Nazis? Yeah, what else is new? The world is full
of assholes. He's exhausted by the prospect of spending
his life fighting them—for once you join the fight, you can't

unjoin. You can't run their guns in the fog once and expect
to get your slacker life back. And then there's his old pal
Walter Brennan, a sometimes deck hand and all times

loveable drunken coot. Who'd watch out for him?
Hoagie sings about grace under pressure. His moody
ballads tend towards jazzy trills designed to lull listeners

into buying more watered-down drinks. When Bacall
sings Hoagie's world-weary lyrics, the place lights up.
Bogie too. He gains another decade of life just by standing

next to her. Even so, he sparks one unfiltered cigarette after
another. Ten years later, unable to shuffle more than
a few steps without collapsing, he will allow Bacall

to stuff him into the household dumbwaiter in order
to lower himself down to the parlor for cocktails with Huston.
Sometimes no one sees the climax coming.

TALKIN' WALPURGISNACHT BLUES

On the day your life suddenly turns noir, you will
spot Robert Mitchum out of the corner of your eye.
He will be leaning against a lamppost, cigarette dangling,
collar open, flies buzzing, and of course heat rising
in waves off the goddamn asphalt. As he crosses the street,
you will think jaguar. You will suspect he is already
circling his prey, already tasting your blood in his teeth.
You will feel your gut instinctively tighten.

On the day your life turns, it may be useful to know
that Mitchum is not always wild, but he is never tame.
The closer he gets, the deeper that dimple in his chin.
When he speaks you may be surprised at the sharpness
of his wit. You may not even know you've been cut
until the blood seeps through your clothing. It may help
to know a few simple things—they won't save you but
they may mitigate the misery as it rolls in like dry lightning.

On that fateful day, you would be wise to avoid a fistfight.
After all, Mitchum's shoulders are not just for show.
He knows how to wrestle the gun from your hand.
And he knows how to take a punch. Once he begins
swinging, he will not stop until all the furniture in the room
is reduced to kindling and the lights in your attic have gone
black. If he backs you into a corner, protect your skull.
Which chair is best to break over his head?

If on that cursed day he decides to give chase, drop
obstacles in your wake. You have about six seconds

to reach your car. Keep the key in the ignition
and your getaway road map in the glovebox.
Expect to drive all night—because he will. Expect
to cross the border with a stolen jalopy on your tail,
Mitchum's face lit dimly by the glow from his dash.
And expect to break a dozen laws while on the run—he will.

On the long day after your life suddenly turns noir,
there will be time to wonder, as the rain beats against
your windshield, just what you've done to deserve this.
Long ago a man called Job lost everything and never
knew why. There's a reason they still tell that story.
Brother, don't you know it. They say the devil wanders
the earth, to and fro, looking for souls to devour. They say
he has a chin carved from granite and a ticking clock for a heart.

After the clouds divide on that day and after smoke begins
to billow from beneath your hood, after you pull off the highway
at some lonely turnout, somewhere, say, south of Vera Cruz,
on a bluff overlooking the Gulf of Mexico, your engine
will sputter and your radiator will run dry. The sun
will reach its peak. You will loosen your collar and lean
against the guardrail. You will light your last cigarette.
What is that sharp odor on the breeze—brimstone?

After everything and everybody in the world, even
the scorpion on the tuck and roll upholstery in
the passenger seat, has joined the cast of your own
private noir, expect the dusty stolen jalopy that's been
on your tail like a hell hound to roll up behind you.
Conjure a pleasant memory if you can. Expect to find

in its place a world of regret. Expect the last sound you hear to be the slow crunch of gravel beneath Robert Mitchum's tires.

ROAD TO OBLIVION

The Ballad of Bob and Bing and Dot

Bob cracks wise while Bing
      croons a ballad to Dot,
who sways her sarong and
      sings a pretty little song
of her own to Bob, who shuffles
      his feet in sawdust
and schemes, meanwhile Bing
      dreams of a desert isle
with Dot beneath a palm,
      his troubles all gone, until Bob
begins to sway and Bing shuffles
      and schemes and Dot dreams,
and don't we all dream the dream
      of that desert isle
where all the people are pretty
      and every joke lands
and the palms protect us from the bombs
      and everybody sings?—
come on now, everybody sing along,
      as the ball bounces from Bob to Bing
to Dot, and back from Dot
      to Bob to Bing, everybody sing!

KARLOFF'S LISP

Difficult to imagine Karloff's
doting mother pampering the tall boy.
But that is how it must have been,
for a lisp such as his can be corrected
with a bit of discipline and a little
instruction and perhaps a healthy dose
of motherly nagging, but she refused,
we must assume, to alter her darling,
whose talent for play-acting and speech-making
delighted and amazed her—her little Boris,
her nascent, shuffling, elegant young monster,
whose hypnotic glare, the glare of body snatcher,
ghoul, and Imhotep followed her from chore
to chore, his sliding sibilant syllables
like smooth-soled slippers across the polished
stone floor of an empty, eerie mansion.

LOONEY TUNES METAPHYSICS

—in memory of Michael Maltese and Chuck Jones

Running the road is the Road Runner's sole
vocation—the source of his joy and serenity.

Above the swirling chaos of his legs,
his head remains still and focused—
his mind alert and his eyes clear.

His only desire is free access to the open road.
The one impediment to his freedom—
the fanaticism of his nemesis.

The Runner's equanimity is the singular
obsession of the Coyote—this he cannot abide.

Coyote's waking hours (his nightmares, too?)
are occupied by surveillance and sabotage.
Constant humiliation does not deter him.

He gives no quarter to doubt. If he admits
the flaw in his doctrine, who then is he?
For what is a Wile E. Coyote if not
a creature of futility? The entire Acme economy
depends upon his perpetual devotion.

To this ongoing desert dilemma, we can only
bear witness. Destined to observe and report,
we cannot free Coyote from his samsara.
We can only laugh. Or cry. Or laugh until we cry.

As gravity pulls Coyote into the canyon
yet again, and the Runner turns
his beak to the camera and blinks, we
in unison join his prayer, crying
from the depths of our being, "Beep! Beep!"

GUINNESS, BLOOD, MARMALADE

—in memory of Peter O'Toole

Presumably it was the Guinness that fueled
an insult, resulting in a late-night fistfight
that caused the flow of blood, prompting
the early morning nostrum of sticky sweetness
spooned on toast and taken with tea.

In those days there were those who posed
in doorways wearing leather jackets
saying *live fast, die young, and leave
a good-looking corpse.* A motto that sounds
more asinine with each passing year.
Hell, with each decade. Such bravado belies
the heart's innate desire for wisdom.

Blame not the nectar of St. James' Gate.
All praise the great Irish tonic's muddy
aspect, earthy scent, creamy head, rich
and frothy essence, suitable for every stage
of life; O praise its bittersweet
tickle-down-the-gullet soul remedy,
a somber pub tune to ward off night-fears
that stalk our lonely homeward walk.

Peter, we stand beside your tombstone
in our tweed and corduroy, lifting
tulip-shaped pints in your honor.
The Galway breezes no longer lift
the flagging banners of our youth,

and we have left our promptbook
for seduction sitting on a rotting log
among trailside shadows; more,
we have lost our lust for violence,
wincing now at the mere thought
of cracked noses and swollen jaws.

For a season we spoke our lines with
such conviction that our troubles
took their bows with or without applause.
Now the theater is empty. The ghost light
glows. Backstage the old manager steps
into the alley, bolts the doors behind him,
and turns up his collar. Like an usher's
fluttering torch, the moon flickers
through the fog, guiding his path home.

NOTES

ONE

"Among Wildflowers"
American poet Emily Dickinson (1830–1886)
composed more than 1,700 lyric poems in her Amherst,
Massachusetts, home. Newspaper editor Samuel Bowles
visited the Dickinson family often. Emily addressed
approximately forty poems and fifty personal letters
to Bowles. English poet Andrew Marvell's (1621–1678)
widely anthologized metaphysical love poem, "To His
Coy Mistress," employs the sun as a metaphor for quickly
passing time as he encourages his beloved to succumb to
his romantic advances.

"Of the Spheres"
Music of the Spheres (or *musica universalis*) was a
metaphysical speculation of the Greek philosopher
Pythagoras, who taught that the movement of the planets
produced harmonious musical tones. Renaissance
astronomer Johannes Kepler believed that such vibrations
could be heard within the human soul. In several modern
spiritual traditions, *musica universalis* is a metaphor for
cosmic unity.

"News of the Flagging World"
The appearance of Miles Davis at the Newport Jazz
Festival in 1955 is widely praised among musicians and
jazz historians as one of the most influential performances
of its era. Winner of Album of the Year at the 1976

Grammy Awards, Stevie Wonder's "Songs in the Key of Life" garnered both critical and popular acclaim. Some cultural historians have proclaimed it the greatest album of popular music.

"Among Swallows"
A Queen of the Ptolemaic Kingdom, Cleopatra reigned from 51–30 BCE. Julius Caesar is alleged to have joined her on a sightseeing Nile cruise of Egyptian monuments. Upon her death, Egypt became a province of the Roman Empire.

"Among Philosophers"
German philosopher Arthur Schopenhauer (1788–1860) is known for his system of philosophical pessimism, a rejection of the German idealism of the previous generation. A later aesthetic theory loosely based on his philosophy promotes the notion that the contemplation of beauty liberates us from the suffering that results from enslavement of the will.

"With the Beatles"
The estate of George Harrison, known as Friar Park, is an eccentric Victorian neo-Gothic mansion located near London in Henley-on-Thames. The current owner is Harrison's widow, Olivia.

"Avoiding the Fate of Old Tiresias"
Blinded by the gods, the Greek mythological figure Tiresias was compensated with the gifts of prophecy and longevity.

"Among Impressionists"
Throughout his career, Paul Cezanne struggled through periods of severe depression and self-doubt, obsessively painting Mont Sainte-Victoire, a 3,317-foot limestone mountain near his home in Aix-en-Provence.

"Among the Heavens"
SpaceX is the popular name for Space Explorations Technologies, the commercial space enterprise of entrepreneur Elon Musk. Its innovative rockets are notable for their vertical take-offs and propulsive landings.

"At the Brown Derby"
Built by Robert H. Cobb (inventor of the Cobb Salad), the derby hat-shaped restaurant in Hollywood, California, was a popular mid-century lunch location for movie stars under contract at nearby studios. Fred Astaire (1899–1987) was an American actor/singer/dancer notable for his elegance, grace, originality, and precision in many RKO and MGM pictures. Astaire functioned as his own choreographer during the golden era of the American film musical.

"Saint Julian and the Rescue Pup"
Julian of Norwich was a fourteenth-century English mystic who authored the spiritual classic, *Revelations of Divine Love*. Her theology is notable for equating divinity with femininity. In one of her visions, she records Jesus as saying, "All shall be well, and all shall be well, and all manner of things shall be well."

THREE

"In Line at Starbucks"
From Norah Jones's debut 2002 album on Blue Note
Records, the phrase, "Come Away with Me," evokes an
ancient trope of romantic rendezvous.

"Music through the Speakers"
A Fred Rose composition from 1947, the Willie Nelson hit
single, "Blue Eyes Crying in the Rain," appeared on his
album, *Red-headed Stranger*, released in 1975. Nelson's
Texas twang was a radio novelty when disco dominated the
music charts.

"Abraham Preparing to Sacrifice His Son"
Marc Chagall's 1936 painting was part of a series of biblical
subjects achieved between 1930 and 1956, when the series
was published in the French art magazine *Verve*.

"The Rooster"
"Le Coq" was painted in Marc Chagall's signature mildly
surrealist manner during his Paris period. Although he was
not an admirer of Sigmund Freud, Chagall nevertheless
enjoyed the prominent visual pun in this 1929 oil on canvas.

"Primary Colors"
I. English Romantic poet William Wordsworth's famous
poem, "I Wandered Lonely as a Cloud," features the
central image of a field of daffodils that he and his sister
Dorothy observed on a walk near the cottage they shared
in the Lake District. Later, Dorothy recorded the image in

her diary. Recent historicist scholarship has emphasized the unacknowledged debt that Wordsworth owes to his sister's talent.

II. Following his friend Carles Casagemas's public suicide at a Parisian café in 1901, Spanish painter Pablo Picasso sank into a deep depression, expressed by a series of monochromatic paintings done primarily in blue and blue-green. The rose period that followed is characterized by happier subjects and warmer colors of southern France.

III. Scottish poet Robert Burns's "A Red, Red Rose" famously compares his love to a rose in full bloom. Bernard Hermann composed the score to Alfred Hitchcock's masterpiece, *Vertigo* (1958). Its haunting themes are among the most memorable scores in American cinematic history. Guillermo del Toro's cinematic Cold War-era fable is saturated with the color green.

"Angel of the Waters"
Designed by Emma Stebbins in 1873, the iconic statue tops Bethesda Fountain in New York's Central Park. The legend of its ancient Jerusalem namesake is found in the New Testament Gospel of John (5:2–9): "Now there is in Jerusalem by the Sheep Gate a pool, which is called in Hebrew, Bethesda, having five porches. In these lay a great multitude of sick people, blind, lame, paralyzed, waiting for the moving of the water. For an angel went down at a certain time into the pool and stirred up the water; then whoever stepped in first, after the stirring of the water, was made well of whatever disease he had. Now a certain man was there who had an infirmity thirty-eight years. When Jesus saw him lying there, and knew that he already had

been in that condition a long time, He said to him, 'Do you want to be made well?' The sick man answered Him, 'Sir, I have no man to put me into the pool when the water is stirred up; but while I am coming, another steps down before me.' Jesus said to him, 'Rise, take up your bed and walk.' And immediately the man was made well, took up his bed, and walked."

FOUR

"Hat Trick"
When a player scores three goals in a hockey game, it's called a hat trick. A natural hat trick is when a player scores them consecutively.

"A Part of the Main"
John Donne: "No man is an island, entire of itself; every man is a piece of the continent, a part of the main. If a clod be washed away by the sea, Europe is the less, as well as if a promontory were, as well as if a manor of thy friend's or of thine own were."

"The Best Thing to Do"
Poets who committed suicide: Anne Sexton, Sylvia Plath, John Berryman, Hart Crane, Seneca, Yukio Mishima, Sara Teasdale, Leopoldo Lugones, Tadeusz Borowski, Vachel Lindsay, Sergei Yesenin, Vladimir Mayakovsky, Virginia Woolf.

"Bitter Crop"
The first concentration camp established by the Nazi party, Dachau (1933–1945), initially housed the party's political

prisoners. The number of Jewish prisoners increased dramatically after Kristallnacht in 1938. American forces of the 42nd and 45th Infantry Divisions liberated the camp in late April of 1945. Two religious memorials, one Jewish and one Christian, now stand at the end of the property where the Disinfection and Medical Experiments barracks once stood.

"Flames"
The Camp Fire of November 2018 devoured the town of Paradise, California, and became a touchpoint in human understanding of the deleterious effects of global warming. Jimi Hendrix's performance at the Monterey Pop Festival during the summer of 1967 launched his short-lived career as a flamboyant and richly talented rock guitarist. The Roman Emperor Nero (who reigned from 54–68 CE) was the first emperor to openly persecute the small religious sect of Christians in the capital city. During the Vietnam War (1954–1975), several young Buddhist monks performed acts of self-immolation in the southern capital city of Saigon as acts of public protest. In the US, Norman Morrison, an American Quaker, imitated their protest beneath the office window of Robert McNamara (Secretary of Defense 1961–1968), considered the architect of US military involvement in Southeast Asia.

"Recluse"
The brown recluse spider (*Loxosceles reclusa*) is a venomous spider found throughout North America, similar to the black widow or the Chilean recluse.

FIVE

"American Femme Fetale"
A classic example of film noir, Billy Wilder's *Double
Indemnity* stars Barbara Stanwyck as an alluring housewife
who seduces an insurance salesman into defrauding his
company by murdering her husband.

"Was You Ever Bit by a Dead Bee?"
Loosely adapted from the Hemingway novel, Howard
Hawks's 1944 *To Have and Have Not* was the first movie
to pair Hollywood veteran Humphrey Bogart with teen
model Lauren Bacall. Despite its otherwise run-of-the-
mill Warner Brothers war-time plot, the on- and off-
screen Bogart/Bacall romantic chemistry and memorable
supporting roles by character actor Walter Brennan and
popular jazz composer Hoagie Carmichael, make this a
classic "popcorn" movie of the era.

"Talkin' Walpurgisnacht Blues"
American film actor Robert Mitchum (1917–1997) became
known for playing menacing characters in several examples
of film noir, including *Night of the Hunter* (1957), *Thunder
Road* (1958), and *Cape Fear* (1962). Talkin' Blues is a musical
cross-genre between folk and country that features a free
melody and rhythmical speech.

"Road to Oblivion"
Bob Hope, Bing Crosby, and Dorothy Lamour made a series of
comic-adventure pictures with musical interludes at Paramount
Pictures during the 1940s. With roots in the Vaudeville

tradition, each "episode" featured Hope and Crosby as con men with Lamour as their love interest. Filled with running gags, exotic locales, Hollywood satire, and improvised verbal sparring, they were wildly popular with war-time film audiences.

"Karloff's Lisp"
Boris Karloff (1887–1969) became famous for playing iconic roles in Universal horror films during the 1930s, including *Frankenstein* and *The Mummy*. With his distinctive voice, he was also a popular radio personality. Late in his career, he was the voice of the Grinch in the animated Dr. Seuss classic, *The Grinch Who Stole Christmas*.

"Looney Tunes Metaphysics"
Michael Maltese (writer) and Chuck Jones (director) collaborated on the Looney Tunes cartoon series *The Road Runner*, which debuted in 1949. In each episode, the ambitious and persistent Wile E. Coyote employs a series of Acme Corporation schemes designed to capture his desert nemesis, the Road Runner, whose clever countermeasures and unwavering Zen-calm demeanor remain consistent throughout the series.

"Guinness, Blood, Marmalade"
Irish actor Peter O'Toole often repeated the following anecdote in television interviews: "Many years ago I sent an old, beloved jacket to a cleaner, the Sycamore Cleaners. It was a leather jacket covered in Guinness and blood and marmalade, one of those jobs . . . and it came back with a little note pinned to it, and on the note it said, 'It distresses us to return work which is not perfect.' So that will do for me. That can go on my tombstone."

ACKNOWLEDGMENTS

The author is grateful to the editors of the following
publications, where some of these poems first appeared:

The Blue Mountain Review: "Occurrence on Bubb Road"
and "Open Letter to the Watchers"

California Quarterly: "Carpe, Fool" and "The Rooster"
(published under the title "On a Painting by Chagall")

Catamaran: "Suburban Hours, VII. Midnight" (published
under the title "Sacrament")

Chiron Review: "A Part of the Main"

Concho River Review: "Abraham Preparing to Sacrifice His
Son" and "Guinness, Blood, Marmalade"

Hiram Poetry Review: "Suburban Hours, VI. Sunset"
(published under the title "Vixen of Kingsbury Place")

I-70 Review: "With the Beatles"

Main Street Rag: "In Line at Starbucks"

Raven's Perch: "Man Beneath a Tree"

Red Wheelbarrow: "American Femme Fetale" and "Was You
Ever Bit by a Dead Bee?"

San Diego Poetry Annual: "Aftermath," "Hat Trick," "Looney Tunes Metaphysics," and "Talkin' Walpurgisnacht Blues"

Still Point Arts Quarterly: "Suburban Hours, V. Afternoon" (published under the title, "Beneath the Holly Oak")

Thanks also to Ken Weisner, Bob Dickerson, Christine Cote, Dorianne Laux, Sally Ashton, and Nils Peterson for their editorial wizardry and friendly encouragement.

ABOUT THE AUTHOR

David Denny is a poet and fiction writer. His books include the poetry collections *Some Divine Commotion* and *Fool in the Attic*, as well as the short story collections *Sometimes Only the Sad Songs Will Do* and *The Gill Man in Purgatory*. His work has appeared in numerous journals and magazines, including *The Sun, Narrative, Catamaran, Rattle*, and *Parabola*. He holds an MFA degree from the University of Oregon. Honors include The Thomas Merton Poetry of the Sacred Contest, The Steve Kowit Poetry Prize, The Center for Book Arts Broadside Award, Silicon Valley Artist Laureate, and numerous Pushcart Prize nominations. He lives in California with his wife, Jill, and their Belgian Shepherd Ginny. More information at daviddenny.net.

SHANTI ARTS

NATURE • ART • SPIRIT

Please visit us online
to browse our entire book catalog,
including poetry collections and fiction,
books on travel, nature, healing, art,
photography, and more.

Also take a look at our highly regarded art
and literary journal, *Still Point Arts Quarterly*,
which may be downloaded for free.

www.shantiarts.com

www.ingramcontent.com/pod-product-compliance
Lightning Source LLC
Chambersburg PA
CBHW070332090426
42733CB00012B/2449